Illustrated by Corinne Randall

Create in me
a pure heart

Bahá'í Prayers

Create in me a pure heart, O my God,

and renew a tranquil conscience within me,

O my Hope!

Through the spirit of power confirm

Thou me in Thy Cause, O my Best-Beloved,

and by the light of Thy glory reveal unto me

Thy path, O Thou the Goal of my desire!

Through the power of Thy transcendent might

lift me up unto the heaven of Thy holiness,

O Source of my being,

and by the breezes of Thine eternity gladden me,

O Thou Who art my God!

Let Thine everlasting melodies

breathe tranquillity on me, O my Companion,

and let the riches of Thine ancient countenance

deliver me from all except Thee, O my Master,

and let the tidings of the revelation of

Thine incorruptible Essence bring me joy,

O Thou Who art the most manifest of the manifest

and the most hidden of the hidden!

Bahá'u'lláh [1]

I am, O my God, but a tiny seed

which Thou hast sown in the soil of Thy love,

and caused to spring forth by the hand of Thy bounty.

This seed craveth, therefore, in its inmost being, for the waters

of Thy mercy and the living fountain of Thy grace.

Send down upon it, from the heaven of Thy loving-kindness,

that which will enable it to flourish beneath Thy shadow

and within the borders of Thy court.

Thou art He Who watereth the hearts of all that have

recognised Thee from Thy plenteous stream

and the fountain of Thy living waters.

Praised be God, the Lord of the worlds.

Bahá'u'lláh [2]

O Thou Who art the Lord of all names

and the Maker of the heavens!

I beseech Thee by them Who are the Daysprings

of Thine invisible Essence, the Most Exalted, the All-Glorious,

to make of my prayer a fire that will burn away the veils

which have shut me out from Thy beauty,

and a light that will lead me unto the ocean of Thy Presence.

Bahá'u'lláh [3]

I testify, O my God, to that whereunto

Thy chosen Ones have testified,

and acknowledge that which the inmates

of the all-highest Paradise and those

who have circled round Thy mighty

Throne have acknowledged.

The kingdoms of earth and heaven

are Thine, O Lord of the worlds!

Bahá'u'lláh [4]

Waft, then, unto me, O my God and my Beloved,

from the right hand of Thy mercy

and Thy loving-kindness, the holy breaths

of Thy favours, that they may draw me

away from myself and from the world

unto the courts of Thy nearness and Thy presence.

Bahá'u'lláh [5]

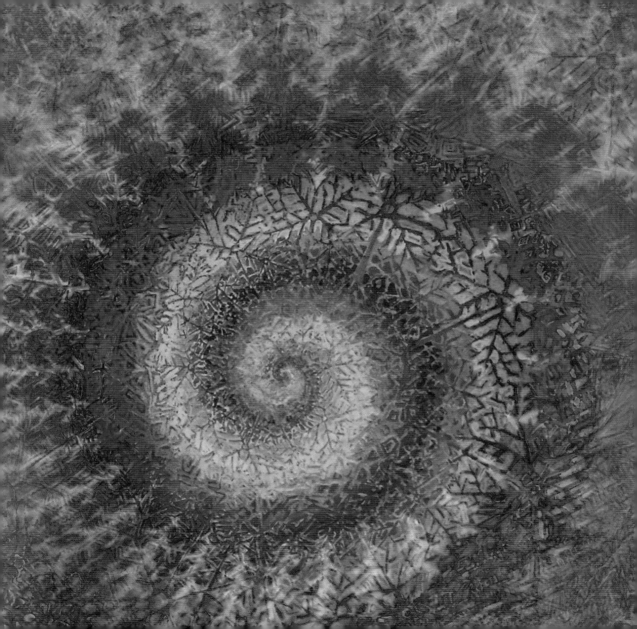

O God, my God! Lowly and tearful,

I raise my suppliant hands to Thee and

cover my face in the dust of that Threshold of Thine,

exalted above the knowledge of the learned,

and the praise of all that glorify Thee.

Graciously look upon Thy servant,

humble and lowly at Thy door,

with the glances of the eye of Thy mercy ,

and immerse him in the Ocean of Thine eternal grace.

'Abdu'l-Bahá [6]

All the atoms of the earth bear witness,

O my Lord, to the greatness of

Thy power and of Thy sovereignty;

and all the signs of the universe

attest the glory of Thy majesty

and of Thy might.

Bahá'u'lláh [7]

He is the Compassionate, the All- Bountiful! O God, my God!

Thou seest me,Thou knowest me; Thou art my Haven and my Refuge.

None have I sought nor any will I seek save Thee;

no path have I trodden nor any will I tread but the path of Thy love.

In the darksome night of despair, my eye turneth expectant

and full of hope to the morn of Thy boundless favour

and at the hour of dawn my drooping soul is refreshed

and strengthened in remembrance of Thy beauty

and perfection. He whom the grace of Thy mercy aideth,

though he be but a drop, shall become the boundless ocean,

and the merest atom which the outpouring of Thy loving

kindness assisteth, shall shine even as the radiant star.

'Abdu'l-Bahá [8]

O my God! O Thou forgiver of sins, bestower of gifts,

dispeller of afflictions! Verily, I beseech Thee to forgive the sins

of such as have abandoned the physical garment and

have ascended to the spiritual world.

O my Lord! Purify them from trespasses, dispel their sorrows,

and change their darkness into light. Cause them to enter the

garden of happiness, cleanse them with the most pure water,

and grant them to behold Thy splendours on the loftiest mount.

'Abdu'l-Bahá [9]

O my God! O my God! Verily, thy servant, humble before the majesty of Thy divine supremacy, lowly at the door of Thy oneness, hath believed in Thee and in Thy verses, hath testified to Thy word, hath been enkindled with the fire of Thy love, hath been immersed in the depths of the ocean of Thy knowledge, hath been attracted by Thy breezes, hath relied upon Thee, hath turned his face to Thee, hath offered his supplications to Thee, and hath been assured of Thy pardon and forgiveness. He hath abandoned this mortal life and hath flown to the kingdom of immortality, yearning for the favour of meeting Thee. O Lord, glorify his station, shelter him under the pavilion of Thy supreme mercy, cause him to enter Thy glorious paradise, and perpetuate his existence in Thine exalted rose garden, that he may plunge into the sea of light in the world of mysteries. Verily, Thou art the Generous, the Powerful, the Forgiver and the Bestower.

'Abdu'l-Bahá [10]

O God! O God! This is a broken-winged bird

and his flight is very slow –

assist him so that he may fly

toward the apex of prosperity and salvation,

wing his way with the utmost joy and happiness

throughout the illimitable space,

raise his melody in Thy Supreme Name

in all the regions, exhilarate the ears with this call,

and brighten the eyes by beholding

the signs of guidance.

'Abdu'l-Bahá [11]

O seeker of Truth! If thou desirest that God may open thine eye, thou must

supplicate unto God, pray to and commune with Him at midnight, saying:

O Lord, I have turned my face unto Thy kingdom

of oneness and am immersed in the sea of Thy mercy.

O Lord, enlighten my sight by beholding Thy lights in this

dark night, and make me happy by the wine of Thy love

in this wonderful age. O Lord, make me hear Thy call,

and open before my face the doors of Thy heaven,

so that I may see the light of Thy glory and become

attracted to Thy beauty. Verily, Thou art the Giver,

the Generous, the Merciful, the Forgiving.

'Abdu'l-Bahá [12]

Magnified, O Lord my God, be Thy Name whereby

the trees of the garden of Thy Revelation have been

clad with verdure, and been made to yield the fruits

of holiness during this Springtime when the sweet

savours of Thy favours and blessings have been

wafted over all things, and caused them to bring

forth whatsoever had been pre-ordained for them

in the Kingdom of Thine irrevocable decree

and the Heaven of Thine immutable purpose.

Bahá'u'lláh [13]

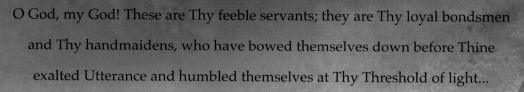

O God, my God! These are Thy feeble servants; they are Thy loyal bondsmen

and Thy handmaidens, who have bowed themselves down before Thine

exalted Utterance and humbled themselves at Thy Threshold of light...

O Lord, shower upon them all the outpourings of Thy mercy, rain down upon

them all the waters of Thy grace. Make them to grow as beauteous plants

in the garden of heaven, and from the full and brimming clouds of Thy

bestowals and out of the deep pools of Thine abounding grace make Thou

this garden to flower and keep it ever green and lustrous,

ever fresh and shimmering and fair.

'Abdu'l-Bahá [14]

O Lord God! Make us as waves of the sea,

as flowers of the garden, united,

agreed through the bounties of Thy love.

O Lord! Dilate the breasts through

the signs of Thy oneness,

and make all mankind as stars

shining from the same height of glory,

as perfect fruits growing upon Thy tree of life.

'Abdu'l-Bahá [15]

O Thou kind Lord! . . .

Gather all people beneath the shadow of Thy bounty

and cause them to unite in harmony,

so that they may become as the rays of one sun,

as the waves of one ocean, and as the fruit of one tree.

May they drink from the same fountain.

May they be refreshed by the same breeze.

May they receive illumination from the same source of light.

Thou art the Giver, the Merciful, the Omnipotent.

'Abdu'l-Bahá [16]

O Thou kind Lord! Unite all.

Let the religions agree and make the nations one,

so that they may see each other as one family

and the whole earth as one home.

May they all live together in perfect harmony.

'Abdu'l-Bahá [17]

O Thou the Compassionate God.

Bestow upon me a heart which, like unto a glass,

may be illumined with the light of Thy love,

and confer upon me thoughts

which may change this world into a rose garden

through the outpourings of heavenly grace.

Abdu'l-Bahá [18]

If it be Thy pleasure,

make me to grow as a tender herb

in the meadows of Thy grace,

that the gentle winds of Thy will may stir me up

and bend me into conformity with Thy pleasure,

in such wise that my movement and my stillness

may be wholly directed by Thee.

Bahá'u'lláh [19]

O God! Refresh and gladden my spirit.

Purify my heart. Illumine my powers.

I lay all my affairs in Thy hand.

Thou art my Guide and my Refuge.

I will no longer be sorrowful and grieved;

I will be a happy and joyful being.

O God! I will no longer be full of anxiety,

nor will I let trouble harass me.

I will not dwell on the unpleasant things of life.

O God! Thou art more friend to me than I am to myself.

I dedicate myself to Thee, O Lord.

'Abdu'l-Bahá [20]

References

1. Bahá'u'lláh, *Bahá'í Prayers,* Bahá'í Publishing Trust, Wilmette, Illinois, 2002, pp.164-165
2. Ibid. p.172
3. Ibid. p.7-8
4. Ibid. p.16
5. Ibid. p.330
6. 'Abdu'l-Bahá, *Bahá'í Prayers,* Bahá'í Publishing Trust, Wilmette Illinois, 2002, p.332
7. Bahá'u'lláh, *Gleanings.* Bahá'í Publishing Trust, Wilmette, Illinois, 1982. p300 CXXXVIII
8. 'Abdu'l-Bahá, *Bahá'í Prayers,* Bahá'í Publishing Trust, Wilmette, Illinois, 1982, pp.133-134
9. Ibid. p.41
10. Ibid. p.41-42
11. Ibid. pp.216-217
12. Ibid. p.61
13. Bahá'u'lláh, *Baha'í Prayers.* Bahá'í Publishing Trust, Rutland Gate, UK. 1975. No.23 pp.29-30
14. 'Abdu'l-Bahá, *Bahá'í Prayers,* Bahá'í Publishing Trust, Wilmette, Illinois, 2002, p.178-179
15. Ibid. p.239
16. Ibid. p.113
17. Ibid.p.114
18. Ibid.p.71
19. Bahá'u'lláh, *Bahá'í Prayers,* Bahá'í Publishing Trust, Wilmette, Illinois, 2002, pp.159-160
20. 'Abdu'l-Bahá, *Bahá'í Prayers,* Bahá'í Publishing Trust, Wilmette, Illinois, 2002, p174-175
    This prayer is attributed to 'Abdu'l-Bahá but the Research Department at the Bahá'í World
    Centre has not yet located any original text and is therefore unable to verify its authenticity.

First published in the USA in 2013
by Intellect, The University of Chicago Press, 1427 E. 60th Street, Chicago, IL 60637, USA

A catalogue record for this book is available from the British Library.

Book Design: Corinne Randall
Publisher: Masoud Yazdani
ISBN 978-1-84150-784-2
Printed and bound by Gomer Press.